THE U.S. ARMY
IN
SOUTH -EAST
SHROPSHIRE
1944

Adrian Turley

Neil Turley

May 2004

Acknowledgements

U.S Army Center of Military History, Washington D.C.
U.S Army Military History Institute, Carlisle, Pennsylvania
U.S National Archives, Maryland
Maxwell Air Force Base, Alabama
Patton Museum of Cavalry and Armor, Kentucky
U.S Army Quartermaster Museum, Viginia

Imperial War Museum

The British Library Newspaper Library
The Bridgnorth Journal

National Monuments Record Centre

Philip C. Grinton Lt.Col. U.S. Army (Retd.)

Clyde Kennedy

Jason F. Morrison

David Englehart
Michael Thompson
Martin Collins
Baron Parkes
Phil Aldridge
Graham Thomas
Barrie Geens
Sheila Lloyd

John Lloyd
Dennis Crowther
Brian Goodman
Simon Oakley
Jane Lawrence
Ken Wallace
Susan Weston

By the same Authors
"The U.S Army at Camp Bewdley and locations in the Wyre Forest"

CONTENTS

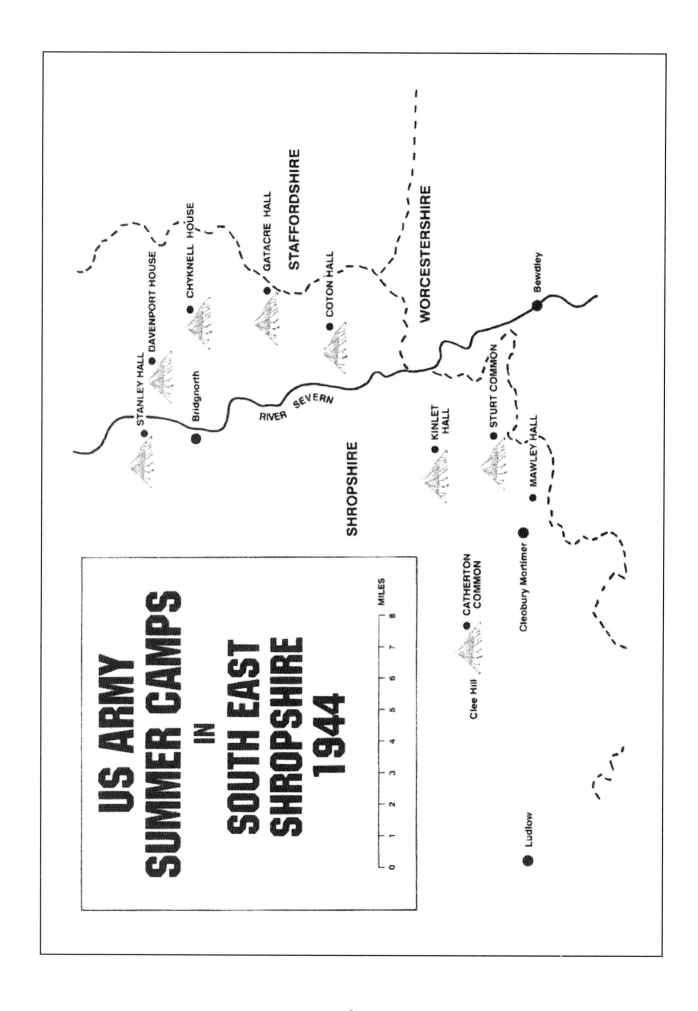

US ARMY
SUMMER CAMPS
IN
SOUTH EAST
SHROPSHIRE
1944

MILES
0 1 2 3 4 5 6 7 8

STANLEY HALL
DAVENPORT HOUSE
CHYKNELL HOUSE
GATACRE HALL
STAFFORDSHIRE
COTON HALL
WORCESTERSHIRE
Bewdley
Bridgnorth
RIVER SEVERN
KINLET HALL
STURT COMMON
MAWLEY HALL
SHROPSHIRE
Clee Hill
CATHERTON COMMON
Cleobury Mortimer
Ludlow

6

Introduction

The 'friendly invasion' of 11/2 million American troops in Britain in the build-up to D-Day (6th June 1944) was probably one of the most complex logistical operations carried out in the history of warfare. Thousands were accommodated in 'winter' or 'summer' tented camps, many of which were constructed in the grounds of stately homes. To accommodate the U.S 90th Infantry Division a group of these tented camps were situated in South - East Shropshire. The Infantry Battalions of the division were quartered at Sturt Common, Kinlet Hall, Gatacre Hall and Coton Hall while the Field Artillery Battalions were quartered in the grounds of Davenport House. Additional camps were at Stanley Hall and Chyknell to accommodate coloured Quartermaster units.

The construction of this group of camps was started by the 373rd. Engineer General Service Regiment. But before they were able to complete the camps they were assigned to more important projects, demanding an organization of a heavy construction background, including the extension of the storage yards and depot at Barry and later building "Phoenixes" (Mulberries) at Tilbury Docks. Their unfinished camp work was taken over by the 95th. and 1310th. Engineer General Service Regiments. These were both coloured units.

Even a tented camp was a major logistical enterprise. A tented camp for 1,250 men required over 200 tents and around 20 semi-permanent buildings for use as mess halls, admin offices, kitchens, bath houses, sickbays, entertainment areas and a guard house. The buildings consisted mainly of 24ft. span Nissen huts and standard Ministry of Works concrete prefabricated huts. A camp of this capacity would be spread over about 40 acres.

Turf removed in preparation of the foundations of the buildings was often used for camouflaging the Nissen huts.

The majority of the troops arriving in Britain landed at Gourock and Greenock on the Clyde or Liverpool. They were then transported by train to a railhead close to their intended camp. The detraining stations for the camps in South East Shropshire were Bewdley, Bridgnorth, Albrighton and Coalport (LMS).

60 years on little or no evidence remains of these camps, the sites of which are all on private property.

After the departure of the U.S troops during August 1944 most of the camps were used as prisoner of war camps housing German or Italian prisoners. Other camps we used to accommodate displaced persons.

U.S TROOPS ARRIVE AT LIVERPOOL

The "Dominion Monarch" arriving alongside the landing stage at Liverpool. 4 April 1944 with U.S Army troops including the 357th Infantry Regiment and the 343rd Field Artillery Battalion en route to tented camps at Kinlet, Gatacre and Davenport House.

Imperial War Museum H37380

The "Athlone Castle" arriving at Liverpool 4 April 1944 with U.S Army troops including the 345th and 915th Field Artillery Battalions en route to the tented camp at Davenport House.

Imperial War Museum H37394

8

American troops on the landing stage after disembarking from the "Dominion Monarch" at Liverpool, 4 April 1944.

Imperial War Museum H37390

American troops boarding a waiting train at Liverpool. 4 April 1944

Imperial War Museum H37400

Principal Troop Movements from Ports to Tented Camps in South East Shropshire

Arrival date	Unit	Camp	Arrival port	Ship
4 April 1944	357 Infantry Regiment	Gatacre Kinlet Hall	Liverpool	Dominion Monarch
	343 Field Artillery Battalion	Davenport	Liverpool	Dominion Monarch
5 April 1944	345 Field Artillery Battalion	Davenport	Liverpool	Athlone Castle
	915 Field Artillery Battalion	Davenport	Liverpool	Athlone Castle
6 April 1944	445 Q.M Truck Company	Chyknell		
	447 Q.M Truck Company	Stanley Hall		
	448 Q.M Truck Company	Stanley Hall	??	??
	642 Q.M Truck Company	Chyknell		
	3200 Q.M Service Company	Stanley Hall	Greenock	Brazil
	3201 Q.M Service Company	Stanley Hall	Greenock	Brazil
7 April 1944	221 Signal Depot Company	Mawley Hall	Gourock	Queen Elizabeth
8 April 1944	344 Field Artillery Battalion	Davenport	Liverpool	John Ericsson
	358 Infantry Regiment	Sturt Common Coton Hall	Liverpool	John Ericsson
26 May 1944	3918 Q.M Gasoline Company	Chyknell		
	3919 Q.M Gasoline Company	Chyknell	??	??
	3920 Q.M Gasoline Company	Chyknell		
13 June 1944	999 Field Artillery Battalion	Stanley Hall	Greenock	Nieuw Amsterdam
29 June 1944	240 Field Artillery Battalion	Gatacre	Gourock	Queen Elizabeth
30 June 1944	3 Cavalry Group	Kinlet Hall	Greenock	Aquitania
	43 Cavalry Recn. Squadron	Kinlet Hall		
4 July 1944	166 Engineer C Battalion	Sturt Common	Greenock	West Point
6 July 1944	135 Engineer C Battalion	Davenport	Greenock	West Point
	167 Engineer C Battalion	Sturt Common	Liverpool	Mauretania
	248 Engineer C Battalion	Sturt Common	??	??
14 July 1944	253 Field Artillery Battalion	Kinlet Hall	Liverpool	Columbie
	274 Field Artillery Battalion	Davenport	Liverpool	John Ericson

  At the beginning of May 1944 there were approximately 21,600 U.S troops in Shropshire as a whole, of which 11,000 were in the group of camps in the area covered by this book.

Photographs of tented camps in occupation are extremely rare.
This photograph shows troops queuing for their 'chow' at a typical tented camp somewhere in the south of England.

Photo : National Archives

11

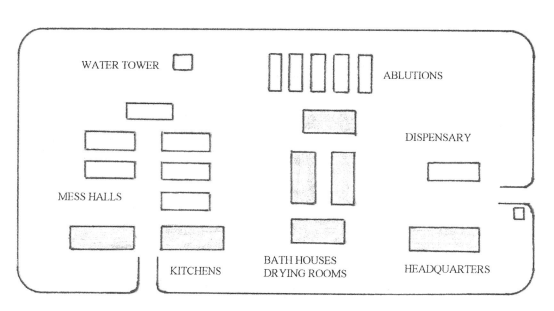

WATER TOWER

ABLUTIONS

DISPENSARY

MESS HALLS

KITCHENS

BATH HOUSES
DRYING ROOMS

HEADQUARTERS

TYPICAL LAYOUT OF COMMUNAL BLOCK
FOR TENTED CAMP

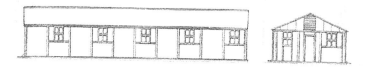

Ministry of Works standard prefabricated building
used for mess halls.

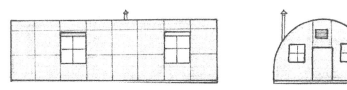

Nissen Hut
Used for kitchens, bath houses, drying rooms and headquarters

Pyramidal, 6 man, tents

12

STURT COMMON

Sturt Common posed a difficult siting problem because of the hilly location, but was most efficiently handled by Company B of the 373rd. Engineer General Service Regiment under the Company Commander, 1st Lt. Clement E. Powell, CE. The nearest town was Bewdley (North Wales Engineer District). The two 1250 man communal blocks were separated by a large aqueduct, supplying water to Birmingham, which had to be protected. Twenty three per cent progress on the double job was reported from the start on 3 December 1943 to 31 December 1943, during which time Company B put in 19,628 man hours, only 25% of the company strength being used on other than construction duties. On 12 January 1944, the project as a whole was 41% complete and turned over at that time to the 95th. Engineer General Service Regiment, which was a coloured unit.

On completion of the camp a detachment of the 295th Replacement Company arrived to carry out guard duties until the arrival of the advance detachments of the 90th Infantry Division on 29 March 1944.

The 2nd and 3rd Battalions and Special Units of the 358th Infantry Regiment arrived at Bewdley station on 8 April 1944 and were brought to Sturt Common by truck.

Training began immediately with special emphasis on physical conditioning exercises and marches over the picturesque English countryside. Daily the men were required to carry full combat equipment on fast road marches. Another hike was added to the busy schedule for some when they set out for the nearby towns of Kidderminster and Bewdley, where the local atmosphere as well as ale was absorbed.

Elements of the 90th Infantry Division quartered at Sturt Common were as follows :
    315th Medical Battalion, Company B
    358th Infantry Regiment Headquarters
    358th Infantry Regiment, Headquarters Company
    358th Infantry Regiment, 2nd Battalion Headquarters
    358th Infantry Regiment, 2nd Battalion, Headquarters Company
    358th Infantry Regiment, 2nd Battalion, Company E
    358th Infantry Regiment, 2nd Battalion, Company F
    358th Infantry Regiment, 2nd Battalion, Company G
    358th Infantry Regiment, 2nd Battalion, Company H
    358th Infantry Regiment, 3rd Battalion Headquarters
    358th Infantry Regiment, 3rd Battalion, Headquarters Company
    358th Infantry Regiment, 3rd Battalion, Company I
    358th Infantry Regiment, 3rd Battalion, Company K
    358th Infantry Regiment, 3rd Battalion, Company L
    358th Infantry Regiment, 3rd Battalion, Company M
    358th Infantry Regiment, Anti-Tank Company
    358th Infantry Regiment, Cannon Company
    358th Infantry Regiment, Medical Detachment
    358th Infantry Regiment, Service Company

The 358th Infantry Regiment departed from Sturt Common on 12 May 1944 by road transport to an embarkation camp at Llanmartin near to the port of Newport.

A road being worked on at Sturt Common. Various layers go into road construction – cinders, hardcore (broken rock) and gravel.

A partition is installed as bricklayers work in enlisted men's bath house.
Photos : 373 Engineer General Service Regiment / National Archives

With the ribs joined and the end section assembled, erection is started on a kitchen building.
Company B, 373rd Engineers. 6 January 1944.

Framework is installed in the erection of a kitchen building by Company B. 6 January 1944.
Photos : 373 Engineer General Service Regiment / National Archives

166th Engineer (C) Battalion

Commanding Officer : Lt. Col. Olen B. Curtis

The following is an extract from the history of the 166th Engineer (C) Battalion ;

On the 26th June 1944, with everything we owned either on our backs or in our duffle bags, which we were carrying, we departed by train from Camp Myles Standish, Mass, for the Boston Port of Embarkation. Upon arrival at the pier we were given doughnuts and coffee by the American Red Cross while a Navy band played for us. After a wait of about an hour we boarded our ship the U.S.S 'West Point'. The next morning at 0450 hours while everyone was still slumbering anchor was hoisted and we officially began drawing our 20% extra. The trip across was very pleasant and everyone seemed pleased to enjoy themselves as much as possible under the circumstances. Later on we heard that several nights out from port we had to change our course because of submarines but it was never confirmed. On the 3rd July we steamed up the Firth of Clyde and dropped anchor just off Greenock, Scotland. Another night was spent aboard ship and early next morning the big task of unloading began. Immediately after landing at Greenock everyone was put on board a train, where we were again given doughnuts and coffee by the Red Cross, and departed for bonny England.

Late in the afternoon of the 4th July we arrived at Bewdley, where we found trucks waiting to transport us to camp. About an hour after leaving the train we found ourselves at our new home, Camp Sturt Common, Shropshire County, England. We immediately began unloading our personal equipment and moving into large tents in which we were to live during our stay.

When we arrived at camp we were transferred to the Third United States Army commanded by Lieutenant General George S. Patton, Jr, better known as " Blood and Guts" to all the men and attached to the 1117th Engineer Combat Group. The Third Army at the time was massing its troops for preparation in crossing to the continent. We were kept pretty busy during our stay at Sturt Common drawing our Engineer equipment, ordnance equipment and having various inspections of different items to assure against shortages. The lettered companies spent a week near Oxford attending a Bridge school. While there several floating Bailey Bridges were constructed and torn down over the Thames River.

The Battalion was highly in favour of keeping up the morale of the men, which was excellent at this time, so several tours were arranged to various points of interest for the men so desiring to go. Several times we were fortunate enough to secure seats in the famous Shakespearian theater at Stratford on Avon to see the Shakespearian plays Hamlet and Macbeth.. In addition passes were issued to visit the nearby towns of Bewdley, Stourport and Kidderminster. It was while we were stationed here that we learned to respect the English more than we were accustomed to.

Eventually all good things must come to an end so we departed from Sturt Common on the morning of the 4th August 1944 for Camp D-7, Dorchester, arriving there the same afternoon after travelling a distance of 150 miles. There was not much to do so the men just relaxed for a couple of days. The morning of the 6th found us again on the move, this time with our destination as Portland. Upon arrival we boarded LST's to cross the channel to the continent. On the morning of the 7th August we arrived at Utah Beach, France.

....

248th Engineer Combat Battalion

Commanding Officer : Major Elbert R. Taylor

Arrived Sturt Common 6 July 1944
Departed Sturt Common 21 July 1944
Boarded LST at Portland 25 July 1944 for France

Strength of Battalion : 29 Officers, 3 Warrant Officers and 603 Enlisted Men.

....

The Wagons Received book from the GWR station at Arley records the arrival on 12 July 1944 of 5 wagons of Government Stores from Glasgow for the U.S Army.
These stores were probably for the Engineer Combat Battalions at Sturt Common.

167th Engineer (C) Battalion

Commanding Officer : Major Emmett J. Manion Jr.

The following is an extract from the history of the 167th Engineer (C) Battalion:

On the 26th June 1944, the battalion proceeded by rail from Camp Myles Standish, Massachusetts, to the Boston Port of Embarkation, and boarded the British ship 'Mauretania'. The battalion was chosen as the unit to assist the crew in handling the work details aboard the ship. Major Manion was appointed the ship's executive officer, and Major MacCord was the provost marshal. The battalion furnished the guards to police the boat and also gunners to assist the crew in manning the ship's guns. The boat left Boston harbor on 28th June, destination unknown. No rough seas or bad weather was encountered during the voyage. The battalion was highly praised and complimented for its fine work done aboard ship. The ship docked at Liverpool, England on 5th July 1944.

On 6th July 1944, the battalion disembarked from the Army Transport at 1300 and proceeded by rail from Liverpool to Sturt Common, England, arriving there at 2045. *

On arriving at Sturt Common the battalion was attached to the 1117th Engineer Combat Group assigned to Third Army. The battalion was notified that it was to have some intensive training in mines and booby traps, floating bridges and aircraft identification.

On 9th July 1944, Company A left Sturt Common by motor convoy at 1130 arriving at Pangbourne at 2100, vicinity of the Thames River. The Company bivouaced here for one week, training in the construction of the floating Bailey Bridge. The Company left Pangbourne by motor convoy at 1745 on 17th July for Sturt Common.

During the stay in England, the battalion immediately started work on obtaining supplies and also a review of training subjects.

Company B and Company C trained at Pangbourne during the following weeks in the construction of the floating Bailey Bridge. Officers and enlisted men were sent to specialist schools for specialised training in camouflage, mines and booby traps, engineer bridge schooling and communications training.

On 3rd August 1944, the battalion departed from Sturt Common for the Marshalling Area at Camp G-3 and embarked on LST 402 at Southampton on 4th August 1944, disembarking at Utah Beach 1530 0n 5th August.

The unit strength on arrival at Sturt Common was 32 Officers and 602 Enlisted Men.

* The train arrived at Bewdley station pulled by LMS 4-6-0 Class5 locomotive No.5308 .

Photo courtesy : English Heritage (NMR)

Aerial photograph of Sturt Common
30 September 1948

KINLET HALL

Although troops moved to this project on 29 November 1943, it was not possible to commence work until 4 December 1943 because no plans or specifications were available. During the month of December Company A of the 373rd. Engineer General Service Regiment, under the command of Capt. T.S.Parsons, CE, expended 26,174 man hours on this project. At the start, the water tanks and tower pipe fittings, plumbing and electrical stores and fixtures, 24-feet Nissen Huts and Ministry of Works type huts were not available. The design and accommodations were set up for a summer tented camp for 2500 men. The first housing material arrived on 15 December, it was only then that it was possible to start the semi-permanent structures. Total completion on the double project as a whole amounted to 26% on 11 January 1944, when the project was turned over to the 95th. Engineer General Service Regiment.

On completion of the camp a detachment of the 295th Replacement Company arrived to carry out guard duties until the arrival of the advance detachments of the 90th Infantry Division on 29 March 1944.

The 2nd and 3rd Battalions of the 357th Infantry Regiment arrived at Bewdley station by troop trains from Liverpool on 5 April 1944 and thence by truck to Kinlet.

Elements of the 90th Infantry Division quartered at Kinlet were as follows :

  315th Medical Battalion, Company D
  315th Engineer Combat Battalion, Company B
  357th Infantry Regiment Headquarters
  357th Infantry Regiment, Headquarters Company
  357th Infantry Regiment, 2nd Battalion Headquarters
  357th Infantry Regiment, 2nd Battalion, Headquarters Company
  357th Infantry Regiment, 2nd Battalion, Company E
  357th Infantry Regiment, 2nd Battalion, Company F
  357th Infantry Regiment, 2nd Battalion, Company G
  357th Infantry Regiment, 2nd Battalion, Company H
  357th Infantry Regiment, 3rd Battalion Headquarters
  357th Infantry Regiment, 3rd Battalion, Headquarters Company
  357th Infantry Regiment, 3rd Battalion, Company I
  357th Infantry Regiment, 3rd Battalion, Company K
  357th Infantry Regiment, 3rd Battalion, Company L
  357th Infantry Regiment, 3rd Battalion, Company M
  357th Infantry Regiment, Anti-Tank Company
  357th Infantry Regiment, Cannon Company
  357th Infantry Regiment, Medical Detachment
  357th Infantry Regiment, Service Company

Intensive training was begun immediately with stress being placed on speed marches with heavy loads of weapons and ammunition. Covering 5 miles on foot in less than an hour was the way it went. This can and will be appreciated by those readers who have walked up the steep English hills and who realise that the average rate of march for foot troops is only 21/2 miles per hour.

During their stay at Kinlet Park the men were givenshort passes to nearby towns.

These soldiers, however, were not here for fun, but for the most serious business they had ever undertaken —— and they knew it. Besides, when evening came, a few hours rest is what they wanted most.

The 357th Infantry Regiment departed from Kinlet Park on 13 May 1944, by road, to an embarkation camp at Chepstow.

....

After the departure of the 357th Infantry Regiment further units arrived , in transit, at Camp Kinlet. These were as follows :

3rd Cavalry Group & 43rd Cavalry Rcn Squadron

Advance detachment arrived 6 June 1944.
Main body arrived on the Clyde aboard the liner "Aquitania" on 29 June 1944. The Group and its Squadron arrived at Kinlet the following day.

Strength of Group :15 Officers and 57 Enlisted Men.
Strength of Squadron :38 Officers, 3 Warrant Officers and 733 Enlisted Men.

Departed from Kinlet 13 July 1944, arrived in France 9 August 1944.

253rd Armored Field Artillery Battalion

Strength of Battalion : 33 Officers, 2 Warrant Officers and 488 Enlisted Men.

Arrived Kinlet 14 July 1944.
Attached to 40th Field Artillery Group and XV Corps.
Departed Kinlet 16 August 1944 to marshalling area on south coast prior to boarding LST 517 and LST 529 for Utah Beach, France.

Camp entrance and newly constructed access road. Captain Walter I. Farmer is standing on roadway

Grading work in progress on one of the camp roads. Work done by Company A, 5 January 1944.
Photos : 373 Engineer General Service Regiment / National Archives.

Men of Company A carefully remove sod in preparation for foundation for kitchen.

Corrugated liners are being applied in construction of Drying Room.

Photos : 373 Engineer General Service Regiment / National Archives.

Photo :English Heritage (NMR) RAF Photography

Aerial photograph of Kinlet Park
Nissen huts not visible due to turf camouflage
30 September 1948

Local Memories of Sturt Common and Kinlet Camps

Lorry loads of stone were brought from Clee Hill and ashes from Kinlet Pit to make roads on both sites. A steam roller was acquired from Brecon.

When the troops first arrived they were still paid in dollars. Dollars and cigarette brands such as Lucky Strike and Camel were commonplace in the village as farmers sold them fruit and vegetables. The exchange rate was 5s. 2d. to the dollar and locals exchanged their money at the Post Office.

John Lloyd who lived near the camp at Sturt Common as a boy remembers wandering into the camp where an American Officer asked him what he was doing and where he lived. He took him to his office and made out a pass for him. John used it to visit the camp cinema.

The 'Plough' and the 'Horse and Jockey' pubs at Far Forest were frequented by the Sturt Common troops. The 'Eagle and Serpent' at Kinlet was the favourite venue for the Kinlet troops.

The troops were often seen on exercises in the area, they had a firing range at the Kinlet Pit where marks were painted on the old engine house for target practice. They also had two ammunition stores in the Button Oak area where mortar bombs were stored.

The following is an extract from 'Feed my Lambs', a book celebrating 100 years of Far Forest Lea Memorial C of E First School.

One bright light in the children's day at Far Forest School was the American Forces who were based at Sturt Common and Mawley Hall. They often drove through the village most mornings around the time the children arrived for school and would throw 'candies' for them resulting in a scramble to collect as many as possible.

Photo : 373 Engineer General Service Regiment/National Archives

A view of "A" Communal Block, Kinlet. 5 January 1944.

DAVENPORT HOUSE

On 29 November 1943, Company E of the 373rd. Engineer General Service Regiment under the command of Capt. George W. Cearley, CE, began construction of a double camp designed to accommodate 2500 men. Basically it was two of the standard communal blocks for handling double capacity. As in the case of the other camps, the authorised dump truck equipment was insufficient to handle the transportation problems. On 12 January 1944, when the 95th. Engineer General Service Regiment took over the camp was 44% completed.

The 95th. Engineer G.S Regiment completed the project by 20 March 1944 when a detachment of the 295th Replacement Company arrived to carry out guard duties until the arrival of the advance detachments of the Field Artillery Battalions arrived.

Meanwhile, the advance detachments of the Field Artillery Battalions of the 90th Infantry Division sailed from New York on 1 March 1944 aboard the 'Queen Mary' and anchored in the Firth of Clyde in Scotland. They boarded trains which were to take them to Birmingham and the King Edward School, the Headquarters of the 90th Infantry Division.

From the King Edward School a detachment was sent to Camp Davenport to prepare the camp for the arrival of the main body of troops which were to sail into Liverpool at the beginning of April.

At Worfield village, with its ancient church and quaint shops, the local people welcomed the new arrivals with open arms. Favourite venues for the troops were the two pubs, the 'Dog' and the 'Wheel', the latter being used mainly by the officers.

Trucks were available to take the men to Wolverhampton to visit pubs and attend dances.

Elements of the 90th Infantry Division quartered at Davenport House were as follows :

90th Infantry Division Artillery, Medical Detachment
315th Engineer Combat Battalion, Company A

343rd Field Artillery Battalion (105 mm) Headquarters
343rd Field Artillery Battalion (105 mm) Headquarters Battery
343rd Field Artillery Battalion (105 mm), Battery A
343rd Field Artillery Battalion (105 mm), Battery B
343rd Field Artillery Battalion (105 mm), Battery C
343rd Field Artillery Battalion (105 mm), Medical Detachment
343rd Field Artillery Battalion (105 mm) Service Battery

344th Field Artillery Battalion (105 mm) Headquarters
344th Field Artillery Battalion (105 mm) Headquarters Battery
344th Field Artillery Battalion (105 mm), Battery A
344th Field Artillery Battalion (105 mm), Battery B
344th Field Artillery Battalion (105 mm), Battery C
344th Field Artillery Battalion (105 mm), Medical Detachment
344th Field Artillery Battalion (105 mm), Service Battery

345th Field Artillery Battalion (155 mm) Headquarters
345th Field Artillery Battalion (155 mm) Headquarters Battery
345th Field Artillery Battalion (155 mm), Battery A
345th Field Artillery Battalion (155 mm), Battery B
345th Field Artillery Battalion (155 mm), Battery C
345th Field Artillery Battalion (155 mm), Medical Detachment
345th Field Artillery Battalion (155 mm), Service Battery

915th Field Artillery Battalion (105 mm) Headquarters
915th Field Artillery Battalion (105 mm) Headquarters Battery
915th Field Artillery Battalion (105 mm), Battery A
915th Field Artillery Battalion (105 mm), Battery B
915th Field Artillery Battalion (105 mm), Battery C
915th Field Artillery Battalion (105 mm), Medical Detachment
915th Field Artillery Battalion (105 mm), Service Battery

General George S. Patton, Commanding General, U.S Third Army accompanied by General Bradley visited Camp Davenport a few weeks before D-Day.

Photo :Patton Museum of Cavalry and Armor

Tented area - Battery B - 915th Field Artillery Battalion
Camp Davenport – April 1944

Photo : Clyde Kennedy

344th Field Artillery Battalion

Commanding Officer : Lt. Col. Merton Munson

The following is an extract from the History of the 344th Field Artillery Battalion:

On the evening of March 22 we boarded the 'S.S. John Ericsson', formerly known as the Swedish American liner 'Kungsholm'.

After much delay and confusion we finally set sail for the European Theater of Operations, landing in Liverpool , England, on the 9th of April, Easter Sunday, after an extremely quiet crossing.

At the docks we got our first taste of English friendliness, what with their band playing their welcoming themes and the shouting back and forth. While embarking on the train for our new camp the Red Cross handed out coffee and doughnuts and gum to all the boys. When they were through the train gave a mighty shrill blast and off we lurched for our new camp, Davenport, near Wolverhampton.

While we were at Davenport we received all our sectional equipment and everything that was given to us at our Port of Embarkation. We went through a good physical conditioning period and after a month of this sort of training we headed for Sennybridge, South Wales, where we did some firing on the artillery range. During our stay we were in contact with many "Tommies" and learned a little more about them. At the end of a week of firing, out in that typical wet, raw weather that the United Kingdom is so well known for, we headed back to Davenport supposedly to resume our previous training. When we got back we were told to take only that we would need right away for we would be moving out in a few days. Ten days later we moved through several towns on a long motor march down to what is known as a marshalling area, Chepstow, a town close to Newport, on the Bristol Channel.

At once activity was stepped up to a new lively pace. Our wanderings were limited and much paperwork had to be done. Amazingly enough our "Chow" improved greatly, accompanied by such cracks as "fattening for the kill" and many others. Extra classes on first aid, gas, and our own particular jobs were being held, and a few speeches from "Visiting Firemen" telling us that the "chips were down".

In the last few days of our stay at this place no one was allowed in or out of camp. On the 28th May the truck drivers took all the heavy equipment down to the docks and loaded it on the Liberty ships that were to take us to our objective, and the battalion followed on the train, June 1st.

We stood off Newport for at least forty-eight hours while waiting for our convoy to be made up and then sailed down the channel and around Land's End into the English Channel.

On June 4th, a day of much excitement for all of us, we were briefed by our officers. That caused plenty of talk among the boys for we knew that at last we were to get a crack at the much hated enemy. We were to land in France behind the assault division. Two years of patient waiting and now the time had arrived for everyone to prove his mettle.

915th Field Artillery Battalion

Commanding Officer : Lt. Col. James A. Costain

The following is an extract from the history of the 915th Field Artillery Battalion :

On 18 March 1944 we left Fort Dix for the short train ride to Camp Kilmer, New Jersey. After four frantic days of final inspections and showdowns, we moved out early in the morning of 22 March to the docks of New York and boarded the 'Athlone Castle', an English liner. Before dawn on 23 March 1944 the anchor came up, and we slipped through the harbor and took our place in the line of ships filing out to sea. At last we were on our way overseas!

On 5 April, after a reasonable quiet passage, we arrived at Liverpool, England, and went by train and motor convoy to Camp Davenport.

At Camp Davenport we were issued all new equipment, had physical conditioning and section training and tried to master the English monetary system during trips to Wolverhampton, Birmingham and other nearby towns.

During the week 2-8 May 1944 we went to Builth Wells, Wales, for firing practice on the Sennybridge Range. We calibrated our new guns and spent a few nights in the field.

Following the week at Sennybridge we returned to Camp Davenport, made a few last minute preparations, and on 14 May moved to Camp U-87 near Abergavenny, Wales. A residual group of administrative personnel under Mr. Edwin L. Calvin, the Personnel Officer, was left at Camp Davenport.

At Camp U-87 we had final requisitions for equipment filled, figured out loading plans, put garlands in camouflage nets, waterproofed all our equipment, and wondered what was going on in the "War Room", the little white house on the hill with barbed wire and sentries round it.

On 4 June 1944 we moved out once more and boarded four Liberty ships in Cardiff harbor. Headquarters Battery went on MT 228, A Battery on MT 229, B Battery on MT 230 and C and Service Batteries on MT 231. As soon as the ships were loaded they pulled out into the harbor, dropped anchor, and waited.

In the evening of 5 June we moved slowly out of Cardiff harbor and learned for the first time that we were bound for the eastern shore of the Cotentin Peninsular and were to go ashore on the day following D-Day. Major Bob T. Hughes and a small advance party were going ashore on D-Day and would have a rendezvous area for us.

During the period 6 – 10 June 1944 all the elements of the battalion landed on Utah Beach and assembled near St. Mere Eglise. Our first firing position was at Neuville au Plain.

....

A week after landing in France, Lt. Colonel James A. Costain, the Commanding Officer of the 915th Field Artillery Battalion was killed in action.

....

Clyde Kennedy was a Tech. Sergeant with the 915th Field Artillery Battalion, and with a group of officers and enlisted men went to England on an advance party on 1 March 1944 to set up camps in the Midlands for the arrival of the 90th Infantry Division.

Clyde found the countryside around the village of Worfield almost breathtaking with its beauty. He wrote a letter to his parents in which he tried to tell them about the area around Camp Davenport. Extracts from this letter are reproduced below with kind permission of Clyde Kennedy.

"Travelling from our headquarters in Birmingham to the Artillery Camp which we are setting up at Worfield seemed to propel us into a burst of beauty. The landscape became even more beautiful with each passing mile. The road turned into a valley with a side road running to a small village.

"Following a steep road through a ravine that took us up a hill, we came on to the grounds of a magnificent estate called Davenport Hall which covered many acres. The rolling hillsides and valleys were a solid carpet of green grass except for the cultivated fields, and here and there stood majestic old trees that were not yet in leaf.

"In the grounds was a mansion which was built on the flat top of a hill once undoubtedly the elaborate quarters of the nobleman who owned the estate. Now it was an orphanage for those unfortunates whose parents had been victims of the German bombs or had sent them to a safe haven to get them away from the danger zones around London.

"Looking down into the valley from one side of the huge hill, we could see a stream peacefully winding its way. From another side of the hill one could look down toward the small village of Worfield and small hedge-bordered fields.

"Never before in my life had I seen a more beautiful natural park. The green rolling hills, the peaceful stream, the majestic trees, the clumps of woods, the hedge-bordered fields, the beautiful mansion, the ancient village. Certainly this was the most beautiful peaceful place I had ever seen in my life.

"It seemed rather a shame to build an army camp here. But we are thrilled to have such a place as a temporary home for our Artillery Battalions in the United Kingdom.

"We walked round the grounds of the estate and looked up from a valley to the top of a large flat hill where the camp was to be located and visualised the estate as it had been many years before. Then we walked to the top of the hill. We found a footpath that ran to a small white bridge crossing a ravine through which ran the road to the mansion, and we followed it into a clump of woods.

"The path was old and the woods were dense. A tree had fallen across the path and was rotting away. We detoured around it and presently came to a clearing from which we could look down into a valley.

"There at the bottom of the hill was an ancient Anglican church surrounded by a cemetery. Made of stone, it had a steeple and in the tower was a clock that tolled the hours. The church windows were large and designed with biblical pictures of stained cut glass. Most of the tombstones in the cemetery were weathered and some were crumbling. We read inscriptions carved in the stones that were hundreds of years old. Generations had been buried there.

DAVENPORT HOUSE

"We walked through the cemetery and to the church door. Removing our steel helmets, we opened the door and walked in. All was still, we were alone. A musty odour of old things, not offensive, filled the air.

"Shafts of sunlight beaming through the windows brought to life the artistic brilliantly coloured scenes from the Bible. A carpet lay on the floor, we walked up the centre aisle – then stopped. It was so very quiet, the church was so very old, generations of families had worshipped here and their descendants were still coming to worship in the church of their ancestors. Certainly this was a place with which God must be well pleased. We talked in whispers and walked quietly.

"In one corner of the church were two tombs. On the top of each was a horizontally inclined marble figure, one a man and the other a woman, in Elizabethan dress. Under the floor were vaults of people long dead and we stepped across the tablets inscribed with names and dates."

…………………………..

HEADQUARTERS 8608-M

Davenport Hall
11 April 1944..

GENERAL ORDERS FOR THE GUARD:

I. GENERAL INSTRUCTIONS

1. Members of the guard must realize the importance of and the great responsibility involved in guard duty at this station. It is not uncommon for enemy airmen to parachute to earth in this locality. These fugitive soldiers may be expected to obtain allied uniforms, arms and supplies at any cost. Sentries must consider persons approaching the area with suspicion until positively identified as a member of the command.

2. Informal guard mount will be held daily at 1630, on the parade ground west of the Battalion Headquarters building.

3. a. Uniform : Woolen O.D.s, leggings, helmet liner, pistol belt. (outer garment as prescribed by the Officer of the Day).
   b. The Sergeant, Corporals and Privates of the guard will be armed with carbines. The Officer of the Day will be armed with a pistol.

4. Reliefs will be two hours duration, first relief being posted at 1700.

5. Guard will be posted from Guard Mount to reveille on weekdays and for 24 hours on Sundays.

By order of Lt. Colonel COSTAIN:

BOB T. HUGHES
Major, 8608 –M
Bn Ex. & S-1

General Order issued by the Commanding Officer of the 915th Field Artillery Battalion.

343rd Field Artillery Battalion

Commanding Officer : Lt. Col. Ken Reimers

The 343rd Field Artillery Battalion sailed from the New York Port of Embarkation aboard the 'Dominion Monarch' on 23 March 1944 arriving in Liverpool on 4 April.
They entrained for Coalport were they were met by members of the advance party and taken by truck to Camp Davenport, near Worfield in Shropshire.

While at Camp Davenport new equipment was drawn and put into combat readiness. Service practice and battalion firing exercises were held in Wales.

On 14 May the battalion moved to Camp Bulwark, near Chepstow, where final inspections were held. The camp was sealed off on 29 May and all contact with the outside world was lost. On 3 June battalion moved by train from Chepstow to Newport where Liberty ships were boarded. On 5 June the ships moved out of the Bristol Channel and started around the southern tip of England towards France. Dry runs were history and the real test coming up.

345th Field Artillery Battalion

Commanding Officer : Lt. Col. Frank W. Norris

The following is an extract from the history of the 345th Field Artillery Battallion :

We boarded His Majesty's transport 'Athlone Castle' on 23 March 1944. Each of us remembers the food on the Castle, but we expected no picnic. Some of us remember the sea-sickness. However, the trip across the Atlantic was without serious incident; we landed at Liverpool on 5 April. Going straight to Camp Davenport we received twelve brand new M1 Howitzers, tractors and complete new section equipment throughout the battalion. Here we completed our final training with particular emphasis on gunnery and physical conditioning for all men. Our last stop before Utah Beach was Camp Heath, near Cardiff, where their equipment was weatherproofed. On 3 June 1944, a hell of a hot sultry afternoon, we left Cardiff's Heath Camp for the Cardiff Docks. Dressed in cotton underwear, long johns, 1 pair of wool socks, 1 pair of wool impregnated socks, wool O.D. uniform, impregnated fatigue uniform, impregnated shoes, field jacket, full field and rain coat, we marched 5 miles through Cardiff and melted to a stop at the dock area in an aroma surpassing any known odours! The batteries Hq, A,B and Sv, filed aboard the SS Charles C. Jones (MT 209) and C battery boarded the SS Charles D. Poston (MT 210).
Clutching our sack lunch, we learned our assignments, explored the Liberty ship, and found our howitzers and vehicles already waiting for us. After satisfying our curiosity as much as possible, we bedded down for the night on the steel decks and in the holds.

On the early morning of June 6th we sailed and by late afternoon Wales and England slipped out of view. On the morning of June 8th, after a relatively peaceful channel crossing, we steamed into Utah Beach.

135th Engineer Combat Battalion

The following is an extract from the history of the 135th Engineer Combat Battalion

On 26 June 1944 the 135th Engineer Combat Battalion left Camp Myles Standish for Boston Port of Embarkation and boarded the U.S.S.' West Point'. On 27 June 1944 we set sail without convoy and after a good crossing arrived off Greenock, Scotland, during the afternoon of 4 July 1944.

We debarked the following day and entrained, in two sections, for Camp Davenport, Bridgnorth, Shropshire. The entire Battalion, with a strength of 29 officers, 3 warrant officers and 603 enlisted men reached the camp by the morning of 6 July.

From 6 July to the 6 August the unit was given training in the laying and removal of mines and booby traps, it practised with British mines and explosives, constructed fixed and floating Bailey Bridges, and fired weapons on a nearby British range. During this period we were drawing supplies and equipment and preparing to cross the channel.

On the afternoon of 5 August the Battalion was alerted and on the following morning departed, in motor convoy, for a marshalling area near Southampton.

Photo – Clyde Kennedy
Nissen hut at Camp Davenport – April 1944

274th Armored Field Artillery Battalion

The following is an extract from "Longneck",
the History of the 274th Armored Field Artillery Battalion
Reproduced by permission of Jason F. Morrison.

 Longneck

We were ordered by the Third United States Army Headquarters to assume this code identification while we were in England. Once in combat, the word "Longneck" was not only used in connection with our telephone but our route marking sign out of an inspiration furnished by the word. A giraffe head supported on a very long neck with the nose pointing in the direction of travel was placed at obvious points along the route of march by the lead vehicle. This kept our column intact when the interval between vehicles was too great for sight contact.

Everyone was glad to see land after 11 days at sea. We first sighted the north eastern part of Ireland, after the Isle of Man in the Irish Sea and the next day England.. Under the protection of a blanket of P.38's, the S.S 'John Ericsson' docked in South West England about dusk on 13 July 1944. We tied up at the great floating "Prince" dock at Liverpool for the night. In the morning there was a scramble, each man making his horseshoe roll, filling his pack, and struggling to close his duffle bag and drag it on deck. Space for those extra boxes of candy, razor blades, cigarettes, and cookies was not allowed for in the T/E.

After standing around for what seemed like hours in a typical rainy English day, we struggled down the gangplank and into the railroad station where we boarded our train for the journey into the Midlands. No bands played and our welcome committee consisted of doughnuts and coffee provided by the Red Cross canteen.

English trains surprised most of us. The cars are much smaller than ours, seating at the most about 40 men, and freight cars looked to be smaller than a ton and a half truck. But for smooth riding, their trains are fine. No jolts when you start or stop and as smooth riding as many of our streamliners.

The trip across England was very interesting. The countryside was beautifully green and no one could help but notice the red brick houses, each with its own little garden, which were so characteristic of the English countryside. Many of us, too, were surprised to find the towns we passed through practically untouched by bombs, for we had been lead to believe that all England had suffered heavily from attacks by the Luftwaffe.

Our train finally stopped at Albrighton, a small station near Wolverhampton, where a truck convoy took us to some tents in a cow pasture near the village of Worfield – masquerading under the misnomer of "Camp Davenport". This collection of tents, plus a few Nissen huts which served as kitchens, mess halls and headquarters, was our new home.

Many of the facilities of Camp Davenport were definitely more *Continental* than *American.* This was especially true of the sanitary facilities, and few who were there have forgotten the "honey buckets" and the Englishman with his truck who made the too infrequent collections.

The nightly lorry rides for those with passes to Wolverhampton, plus some unauthorised hikes and bicycle rides to Bridgnorth, the stamping ground of the self-styled American Indians, provided most of our recreation. A few men were fortunate enough to receive weekend passes to visit relatives or go to Birmingham, the second largest city in England – however most of us limited our travels to and between the *Butler Arms, Red Fox, Star and Garter, Golden Lamb* and other equally picturesquely named pubs in Wolverhampton and to *The Wheel Inn* near Worfield. Nearly all the men found English girls interested in learning more about Americans, and it seemed that there was always a crowd "waiting for the nightly lorry" to arrive.

We quickly learned the monetary system and the pub system, but for the femininity, each man used his own system. The pound, shilling and pences were straightened out after the first card and crap games. The bitters and stout were clarified after the first drunk; and the woman situation was usually well in hand after the first date.

We were not too impressed at this time when we were notified that we had been assigned to the Third United States Army. Little did we then know the large part that the forces of "Blood and Guts" Patton were to play in achieving final victory in Europe. Most of our working time during this month was occupied with obtaining new equipment and preparing it for action. Everyone, naturally, felt that he could improve the ordnance version of his vehicle and changes at least were made.

Our trip to the *Sennybridge Artillery Range* to calibrate our guns gave us another chance to see parts of rural England and Wales. The route with its many turnings took us through Kidderminster, Hereford, the Black Mountains of Wales, and into the Landovery Hills where the range is located. The "bloody" rain, as usual, dampened our spirits, clothing, vehicles and equipment.

We barely had time to catch our breath after this trip when, on 16 August, we moved to a marshalling area near Southampton, in final preparation for our trip to France. After a night in this area, breakfast and fuelling up with petrol, rations, cigarettes, sea sick pills, "P" bags, gum and "D" ration chocolate, we started out on our way to Weymouth where the battalion was split and loaded into the two LST'S (Landing Ship Tank) *Dorchester* and *Stardust.* That night, the 17th August, we pulled anchor for France, bidding "Cheerio" to Jolly Old England.

ORGANIZATION CHART

274th ARMORED FIELD ARTILLERY BATTALION

Commanding Officer : Lt. Col. Leon Bieri.

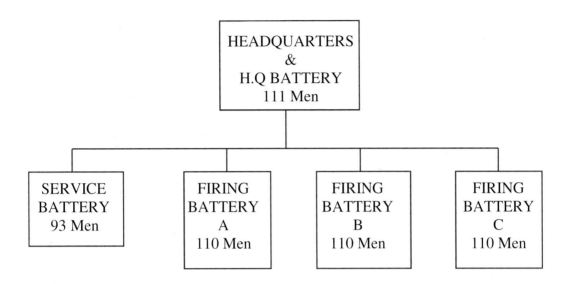

```
                    ┌─────────────────┐
                    │  HEADQUARTERS   │
                    │        &        │
                    │   H.Q BATTERY   │
                    │     111 Men     │
                    └─────────────────┘
```

| SERVICE BATTERY 93 Men | FIRING BATTERY A 110 Men | FIRING BATTERY B 110 Men | FIRING BATTERY C 110 Men |

EQUIPMENT

 18 …. M7 Priest 105mm Motor Howitzer Carriages
  3 ….. M4 Sherman Tanks
 25 ….. 2 1/2 Ton Trucks
 22 ….. Jeeps
 32 ….. Halftracks
 26 ….. .50 Machine Guns
 22 ….. .30 Machine Guns
116 …. Sub Machine Guns
413 …. .30 Calibre Carbines
 40 …. Bazookers
  2 ….. Piper Cub Liaison Planes

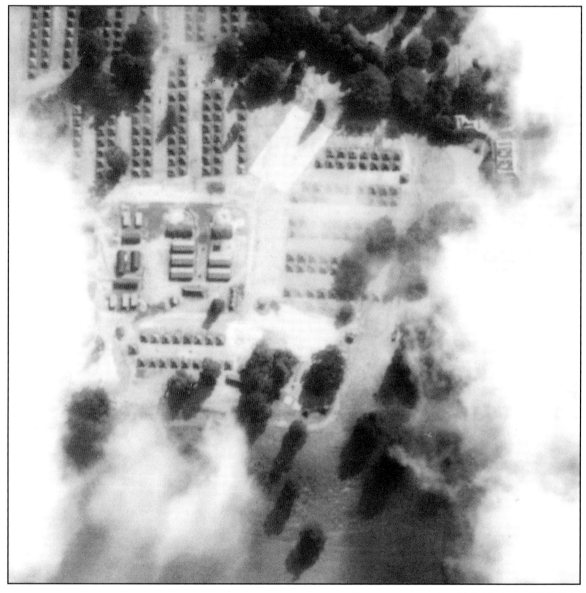

Photo courtesy : English Heritage / (NMR)

CAMP DAVENPORT
Partly obscured by cloud
24 August 1944
Photograph taken by U.S.A.A.F 7th Photographic Group

GATACRE HALL

A 1250 man camp was placed under construction on 26 November 1943 by Company D of the 373rd. Engineer General Service Regiment under the command of 1st Lt. William V. Roedter, CE. This unit was assisted by the 420th Quartermaster Dumper Truck Company. The site was located in the North Wales Engineer District near Bridgnorth.

The work included drainage, water supply, sanitary sewerage, plumbing, electric service and wiring tented structures, messing facilities and heating. Hardcore (broken stone) for the roads was difficult to obtain at this job because of the long hauls. The buildings listed as follows, typical of all tented camps, were erected at Gatacre :

- 2 Kitchens
- 6 Mess Halls
- 5 Ablutions for Enlisted Men
- 2 Bath Houses for Enlisted Men
- 1 Bath House for Officers
- 2 Drying Rooms
- 1 Dispensary
- 1 Headquarters

On 20 December 1943, the 2nd. Platoon of Company C under the command of 1st Lt. Marcus W. Whaley, CE, relieved Company D and assumed responsibility for construction of this camp. On 12 January 1944, after 60% of the work had been completed the 95th Engineer General Service Regiment took over construction of this camp. The 413th Quartermaster Dumper Truck Company also assisted in the completion of the camp.

On completion of the camp advance detachments of the 90th Infantry Division arrived. The main body of troops arrived on 5 April 1944.

Elements of the 90th Infantry Division quartered at Gatacre were as follows :
> 357th Infantry Regiment, 1st Battalion Headquarters
> 357th Infantry Regiment, 1st Battalion, Headquarters Company
> 357th Infantry Regiment, 1st Battalion, Company A
> 357th Infantry Regiment, 1st Battalion, Company B
> 357th Infantry Regiment, 1st Battalion, Company C
> 357th Infantry Regiment, 1st Battalion, Company D
> 315th Medical Battalion, Company A

The 1st Battalion of the 90th Infantry Division departed from Camp Gatacre, by road, on 13 May 1944 to a camp at Chepstow to prepare for overseas movement.

The next known unit to use Gatacre as a temporary transit camp was the 240th Field Artillery Battalion.

240th Field Artillery Battalion

Commanding Officer : Lt. Col. Beverley D. Jones

The following is an extract from the history of the 240th Field Artillery Battalion

On 20 June 1944 the 240th Field Artillery Battalion boarded the largest passenger ship afloat – the 'Queen Elizabeth' of the Cunard Line, converted into a troop transport. The 240th formed but a minute part of more than 15,000 troops aboard for this voyage.

The 'Queen Elizabeth' left New York Harbour at 0700 on 22 June 1944. Then followed six long and boring days at sea, during which the firing batteries manned the anti-aircraft defences of the ship. On 28 June 1944, the 'Queen Elizabeth' dropped anchor in the Firth of Clyde, Scotland. The organization debarked at Gourock, Scotland and at 1600 that day boarded a train which arrived at Bridgnorth, Shropshire at 0730 the following morning.

After arriving at Camp Gatacre, England on 29 June 1944, the 240th Field Artillery Battalion spent the following three weeks on training, drawing of combat supply and formation of its motor pool. Nearby towns visited on pass included Kidderminster, Wolverhampton and Birmingham.

On 8 July 1944, Brigadier General John Lentz, Commanding General of XII Corps Artillery visited the organization at 1100 and departed at 1245.

Finally, on 18 July 1944, the Battalion moved by motor to Camp Bulwark, at Chepstow, Monmouthshire, a concentration area, where last minute preparations for further overseas movement were to be made. At this camp it was learned that the 71/2 ton trucks, supposed to be issued as prime movers for the organization weapon — 155mm Gun — were unavailable, and that M4 tractors would be issued in lieu thereof. Accordingly, personnel were given intensive instruction in the operation and maintenance of the new vehicle.

Strength of Unit : 28 Officers and 508 Enlisted Men.

Names of Battery Commanding Officers:
(1) Hq. Btry. : Captain John R. Brennan
(2) A Btry. : Captain JamesB. Hallums
(3) B Btry. : Captain William M. Hart
(4) C Btry. : Captain Walter F. Tucker
(5) Sv Btry. : Captain Alfred M Olmsted
(6) Med. Det. : Captain John H. Dickenson

COTON HALL

On 29 November 1943, construction of a 1250 man camp was begun by Company C of the 373rd. Engineer General Service Regiment. This camp, also in the North Wales Engineer District, was located near Bridgnorth. This company set up temporary quarters in tents and built 35% of the project during the first months operations, despite the fact that on 20 December, the First Platoon was detached and assigned to Gwernheylod Camp and the Second Platoon was assigned to Gatacre. The water supply point for this camp was at Blunder Bridge on the Bridgnorth Road. The vehicle parks for the area were built directly on sod. All sod removed from building sites was stockpiled for later use as camouflage. On completion of work on 12 January 1944 the records on this project were as follows : Roads 79% ; Vehicle Parks 40% ; Kitchens 23% ; Mess Halls 68% ; Bath Houses 48% ; Drying Rooms 48% ; Headquarters 65%. The 95th. Engineer General Service Regiment took over this project on 22 January 1944.

The 95th. Engineer G.S Regiment completed the project by 20 March 1944 when a detachment of the 295th Replacement Company arrived to carry out guard duties until the arrival of the advance detachments of the 90th Infantry Division on 29 March 1944.

Elements of the 90th Infantry Division quartered at Coton Hall were as follows :
- 90th Quartermaster Company
- 358th Infantry Regiment, 1st Battalion Headquarters
- 358th Infantry Regiment, 1st Battalion Headquarters Company
- 358th Infantry Regiment, 1st Battalion, Company A
- 358th Infantry Regiment, 1st Battalion, Company B
- 358th Infantry Regiment, 1st Battalion, Company C
- 358th Infantry Regiment, 1st Battalion, Company D
- 603rd Quartermaster Graves Registration Company, 3rd Platoon
- 790th Ordnance Light Maintenance Company

On 7 May 1944, General Gilbert Cook, Commanding Officer of XII Corps, visited Camp Coton.

The 1st Battalion of the 358th Infantry Regiment and the other elements of the 90th Infantry Division departed from Camp Coton on 12 May 1944.

The next units to arrive were the 3255th Signal Service Company and the 93rd Signal Battalion. The 93rd Signal Battalion, comprising of 31 Officers, One Warrant Officer and 897 Enlisted Men had previously been stationed at the XII Corps Headquarters at Camp Bewdley. The move to Camp Coton took place on 15 June 1944. The stay at Coton was to be short lived, as both units moved to the south of England on 9 July 1944, prior to duty in Normandy.

Coton Hall had previous connections with the U.S.A. The Hall was the ancestral home of the Lee family for many years. The most famous member of the family was General Robert E. Lee (1807 – 1870), the U.S Confederate leader defeated at the battle of Gettysburg. Henry Lee was another member of the family with links to Coton Hall. He was a signatory of the Declaration of Independence at the birth of the U.S.A.

STANLEY HALL

On 24 November 1943, the first of the camps to be started by the 373rd. Engineer General Service Regiment was begun at Stanley Hall, near Bridgnorth, in the North Wales Engineer District. The initial group on this project was Company F, commanded by Capt. J. Ross Nichols, CE, less the 2nd. Platoon. The completed camp provided washing, bathing, messing, sanitary and recreational facilities for 1250 men. Notable feature of this camp was the water tower and four-inch transite water line. A total of 49,883 man hours were consumed in constructing this camp, or 26,117 less than normally figured for this type of project. Work was completed on 10 March 1944.

295th Replacement Company

On 20 March 1944, the 295th Replacement Company was detailed to duty at Camp Stanley as an interior guard company. The Company with 3 assigned officers, one attached medical officer, 16 assigned enlisted men, 16 enlisted men attached for duty and 199 enlisted men attached unassigned entrucked at Pheasey Farm, Staffordshire at 1300 hours and arrived at Camp Stanley at 1520 hours the same day after travelling a distance of 35 miles. The Company used Camp Stanley as a base and put out detachments at 4 other camps for guard duty. The other camps were Camp Davenport, Camp Coton Hall, Camp Kinlet Park and Camp Sturt Common, all in Shropshire County.

Food was sent from Camp Stanley, in food containers, to the other camps to feed the detachments on guard duty there, and the Medical Officer visited each camp daily. A runner was dispatched daily to the 4th Battalion Headquarters at Pheasey Farm to pick up the usual company distribution of special orders, official correspondence and personal mail.

The tour of guard duty was uneventful except during the first two and a half days when the company had to repair the water main.. This experience proved that there was considerable engineer talent in the company.

By 29 March 1944, advance detachments of the units to be stationed at these camps had arrived and taken over, so the company entrucked at Camp Stanley at 1315 hours with 3 assigned officers, one attached medical officer, 16 assigned enlisted men, 16 enlisted men attached for duty and 199 attached enlisted men, arriving at Pheasey Farm at 1615 hours the same day.

The experiences gained during this guard duty were profitable. Not only did every member of the company learn valuable lessons in actually operating under field conditions, but they also gained new knowledge about leadership, command, supply and co-operation.

The first units to arrive for duty were coloured Quartermaster Transport units. These were :

> 447th Quartermaster Troop Transport Company
> 448th Quartermaster Troop Transport Company
> 3200th Quartermaster Service Company
> 3201st Quartermaster Service Company

3200th Quartermaster Service Company

Commanding Officer : 1st Lieutenant Edward F. Gumpf.

The following are extracts from the history of the 3200th Q.M Service Company :

10 March 1944 the unit left San Bernardino, California via rail for a permanent change of station.

15 March 1944 the unit arrived at Camp Myles Standish, Massachusetts.

23 March 1944 the unit left Camp Myles Standish and proceeded by rail to Boston Port of Embarkation and embarked on the U.S Transport 'Brazil' for overseas duty, leaving the port at 0230 24 March 1944.

3 April 1944 the 'Brazil' docked at the Firth of Clyde, Scotland. The unit debarked on 5 April 1944 and entrained at Greenock, Scotland for a permanent change of station.

6 April 1944 the unit detrained at Albrighton , England and proceeded by truck to Camp Stanley Hall, Bridgnorth, England the same day. The strength of the command on arrival at Camp Stanley was 3 officers and 211 enlisted men.

19 June 1944 the Company left Bridgnorth by rail for Taunton and arrived that day at Tetton Park Camp, near Kingston St. Mary, Somerset.

On 22 June 1944 the Company left Tetton Park for Chandlers Ford via rail, where they detrained and proceeded to a marshalling area prior to embarking at Southampton for further overseas duty. The Company arrived at Beach X, France on 26 June 1944.

3201st Quartermaster Service Company

Commanding Officer : Captain H.M. Svensen.

The following are extracts from the history of the 3201st Q.M Service Company :

On 10 March 1944 the Unit departed by train for Boston Port of Embarkation. Arrived at Camp Myles Standish via Needles, California, Alburquerque, New Mexico, Wichita, Kansas, Cleveland, Ohio. No personnel lost en route.

In staging area, unit was schooled for entrainment for overseas, given additional equipment, and on the last day given 43 replacements for men AWOL.

Unit departed for Boston Port of Embarkation on 23 March 1944 and boarded ship U.S Transport 'Brazil' for unknown destination overseas. Unit spent remainder of month on board ship sailing for unknown destination. Weather was good, and seas not too rough.

After spending eleven days at sea, land was sighted on 3 April and unit disembarked from ship on 5 April 1944 and entrained at Greenock for a new station. On 6 April the unit arrived at Albrighton station, England, and here a U.S Army reception party convoyed unit to Camp Stanley Hall, 2 miles NE of Bridgnorth, where our new station was to be. Our unit was quartered in pyramidal tents, together with three other companies. After arrival at Camp Stanley the unit was notified that it had been assigned to 3rd U.S Army and attached to XII Corps. During April conditioning and training of personnel began.

Extracts from the history of the 3201st Quartermaster Service Company (contd).

During the month of May 1944 the organization, located at Camp Stanley Hall, Bridgnorth, received its vehicles, some additional organizational equipment and the unit was employed in additional training for continental service.

During the month of June the organization continued training in Infantry tactics, airplane recognition, mines and booby traps, in addition to marches two to three times a week. During June this organization also acted as a reception party for several units arriving from the United States at different camps located nearby.

Organizational equipment was marked for shipment to the continent upon 'Alert Notice'. 14 enlisted men were transferred to the 571st Quartermaster Railhead Company.

....

The 3201st Quartermaster Service Company left Camp Stanley at the beginning of July 1944.

....

On 3 June 1944, General Gilbert Cook, XII Corps Commander, accompanied by his two aides, Colonel Hyatt (Quartermaster), Captain Moore (G4 Section) and Captain Binkley (Ordnance Section), inspected the 447th and 448th Quartermaster Troop Transport Companies and the 3201st Quartermaster Service Company at Camp Stanley Hall.

....

447th Quartermaster Troop Transport Company

Authorized unit strength : 5 Officers and 131 Enlisted Men.

Duties at Camp Stanley : Hauling personnel and supplies.

Commanding Officer : Captain Frank Sayner
Platoon Leader : 1st Lt. Andrew M. Crowe
Platoon Leader : 1st Lt. William L. Shaffner Jr.
Platoon Leader : 2nd Lt. J. Leroy Collins
Motor Maintenance Officer : 2nd Lt. Richard G.Paulson

After the departure of these units they were replaced at Camp Stanley by the 642nd Quartermaster Troop Transport Company, which had previously been based at Camp Chyknell, and the 999th Field Artillery Battalion.

999th Field Artillery Battalion

Commanding Officer : Lt. Col. Marion T. Watson

The following is an extract from the history of the 999th Field Artillery Battalion :

On 12 June 1944, the liner 'Nieuw Amsterdam' anchored in the Firth of Clyde, just out from Greenock, Scotland. At 2035 hours on this same day the Battalion started to debark onto ferries, and a short time late the entire Battalion was safely ashore in the United Kingdom. Two troop trains were in the station at Greenock and as soon as the Battalion was loaded, started towards Albrighton Station, England. At Albrighton the Battalion was met by its advance party – Captain Monroe S. Bressler, WO.JG Hershal A Davis and Private Edgar Sonier. From Albrighton the Battalion was transported by a Quartermaster Trucking Company to Camp Stanley Hall, about two miles north east of Bridgnorth, Shropshire County, England.

At Camp Stanley the Battalion resumed training and began to draw its T/O equipment. After arrival the Battalion was assigned to the Third United States Army.

On 1 July, the Battalion lost the service of one of its most capable officers when Major Spencer C. Suber, Battalion Executive, was hospitalised with pneumonia and transferred to the Detachment of Patients at the 52nd General Hospital at Wolverley.

Having received instructions to proceed to concentration and marshalling areas in Southern England, the Battalion left Camp Stanley at 1345 hours on Saturday 8 July 1944.

…………………..

Further units to arrive at Camp Stanley were as follows:
>   5th Quartermaster Battalion (Mobile)
>   26th Quartermaster Battalion (Mobile)
>   122nd Quartermaster Battalion (Mobile)

These were coloured transport units which remained at Camp Stanley for a very short time.

After these units had departed the only remaining unit was the 642nd Troop Transport Company.

642nd Quartermaster Troop Transport Company

This unit moved from Camp Chyknell to Camp Stanley during the early part of July 1944.

The following is a record of their duties at Camp Stanley during August.

1 August 1944

Organization notified to be prepared for overseas shipment at a later date. 48 trucks dispatched at 1400 to Supply Depot O.640 (Tidworth) to pick up equipment to be taken overseas.

2 August 1944

Trucks returned at 1800 loaded with equipment.

3 August 1944

Preparation for overseas movement continued by checking vehicles to ensure that they are in proper working condition. The entire day was spent on maintenance work.

4 August 1944

While mechanics were painting code numbers on vehicles and equipment the men were given a showdown inspection for clothing and shortages were requisitioned. Captain Lanfear left for London to deliver secret papers.

5 August 1944

Individual equipment inspection and tool inspection were conducted today. Captain Lanfear returned from London. Camouflage nets and material were received.

6 August 1944

The entire day was spent in preparing camouflage nets which turned out to be a slow and tedious job. The 10 additional gas cans allotted for each truck were filled and put on the trucks.

7 August 1944

Work continued on camouflage nets.

8 August 1944

Camouflage nets were completed. Enlisted men loaded up their equipment on the trucks and had a trial run. Everything went off very smooth.

9 August 1944

Policing the camp area was the main occupation of the day.

10 August 1944

The men again policed the camp. All equipment and personal effects were left on the trucks for preparation for move tomorrow morning.

11 August 1944

Company Reveille was at 0500. Breakfast at 0515. Final police up of the camp was conducted and the Company left Camp Stanley Hall at 0745 en route to new destination in the embarkation area.

Private Fleming stands guard at the site entrance of Company F project.
Here a country lane was converted into a fine heavy duty access road for a 1250 man
camp. 10 January 1944.

Steam roller packs vehicle park, one of two such vehicle areas in this camp. 10 January
1944.

Photos : 373 Engineer General Service Regiment / National Archives

A portion of the communal block at Stanley Hall. 10 January 1944.

Water tower, of brick and steel construction, is an addition to the skyline at Camp Stanley Hall. The encampment is virtually complete in this picture of 5 March 1944.

Photos : 373 Engineer General Service Regiment / National Archives.

Sergeants inspect the interior of Officer's Bath House.
From left to right : Sgt. Hendricks, Sgt. Ronzone of Company F and Sgt. Kirton of the British Royal Engineers.

Water supply presented the problem of piping it a distance of 9,800 feet through rough country. Here a concrete aqueduct carries the 4 inch transite pipe over a small stream. Flush valve is at the left hand of the aqueduct.

Photos : 373 Engineer General Service Regiment / National Archives.

Portion of main camp road is shown in this picture. Personnel tents can be seen on the right.
13 February 1944

Interior view of kitchen.

Photos : 373 Engineer General Service Regiment / National Archives.

Photo courtesy English Heritage (NMR)

CAMP STANLEY HALL   24 AUGUST 1944
Photograph taken by U.S.A.A.F 7th Photographic Group.

CHYKNELL

Chyknell, near Claverley, was a 1250 man summer camp originally undertaken by Company F of the 373rd Engineer General Service Regiment. Work started on 28 December 1943, and halted on 11 January 1944. Only about 3% progress was achieved when the 95th Engineer General Service Regiment, a coloured unit, assumed responsibility on 11 January 1944.

On completion of the camp during March 1944, advance detachments of coloured Quartermaster Transport units arrived. The main body of troops arrived at Chyknell on 6 April 1944. These were as follows:

> 642nd. Quartermaster Troop Transport Company
> 445th. Quartermaster Troop Transport Company
> 3918th. Quartermaster Gasoline Supply Company
> 3919th. Quartermaster Gasoline Supply Company
> 3920th. Quartermaster Gasoline Supply Company

....

GMC 2 1/2 ton truck

642nd Quartermaster Troop   Transport Company

Authorized unit strength : 5 Officers and 131 Enlisted Men.

Duties at Camp Chyknell : Hauling personnel and supplies.

Commanding Officer : Captain Joseph P. Lanfear
Platoon Leader : 1st Lt. Robert P. Butts
Platoon Leader : 1st Lt. James J. Woolley
Platoon Leader : 2nd Lt. Bertram W. Challis
Motor Maintenance Officer : 2nd Lt. Maurice J. Kane

On 3 June 1944, General Gilbert Cook, XII Corps Commander, accompanied by his two aides, Colonel Hyatt (Quartermaster), Captain Moore (G4 Section) and Captain Binkley (Ordnance Section) inspected the 642nd Quartermaster Troop Transport Company.

Early in July the 642nd Quartermaster Troop Transport Company moved to nearby Camp Stanley. (See page 46)

....

T/5 uses level to check alignment of batter boards.

Operations tent and foundations, 8 January 1944.

Photos : 373 Engineer General Service Regiment / National Archives.

Members of 3rd Platoon, Company F,
lay foundation of Nissen Hut.
8 January 1944.

Photo : 373 Engineer General Service
Regiment / National Archives.

Photo : English Heritage (NMR)

Camp Chyknell partly obscured by cloud, 20 April 1944.
Photograph taken by U.S.A.A.F 7th Photographic Group.

3918th Quartermaster Gasoline Supply Company

Commanding Officer : Captain Edward Peyser

Strength of unit : 3 Officers and 123 Enlisted Men

The unit departed from Camp Myles Standish, Massachusetts, on 12 May 1944 arriving at Boston Port of Embarkation the same day. Departing from Boston the following day they arrived at Camp Chyknell on 26 May 1944 and departed for Utah Beach on 13 July 1944.

....

3919th Quartermaster Gasoline Supply Company

Commanding Officer : Captain Glenn G. Bailey

Strength of unit : 3 Officers and 125 Enlisted Men

The unit departed from the Camp Myles Standish, Massachusetts, on 12 May 1944 arriving at Boston Port of Embarkation the same day. Departing from Boston the following day they arrived at Camp Chyknell on 26 May 1944. They departed from Chyknell on 13 July, landing on Utah Beach on 15 July 1944.

> Sgt. William Walker, a member of the 3919th Quartermaster Gasoline Supply Company was formerly with the Harlem Globe Trotters Professional Basketball Team.

....

3920th Quartermaster Gasoline Supply Company

Commanding Officer : Captain Tebay

Strength of unit : 4 Officers and 120 Enlisted Men

The unit departed from Camp Myles Standish, Massachusetts, on 12 May 1944 arriving at Boston Port of Embarkation the same day. Departing from Boston the following day they arrived at Camp Chyknell, Shropshire, England on 26 May 1944.

The unit departed from Camp Chyknell, by road, on 8 July 1944 arriving at a marshalling area at Camp 88, Codford Downs, England. They landed at Utah Beach on 22 July 1944.

....

Duties of Quartermaster Gasoline Supply Company

1. Deliver gasoline and lubricants to units in the field.
2. Procure gasoline from tanks at bulk reduction point.
3. Break down into 5 gallon containers.
4. Set up distribution points in Corps or Division area.

Equipment for each Gasoline Supply Company

17 .... 21/2 ton cargo trucks
17 .... 1 ton, 2 wheel cargo trailers
 3 .... 1/4 ton trucks
 5 .... 3/4 ton weapon carrier trucks
 3 .... 21/2 ton, 750 gallon tank trucks

21/2 ton,, 750 gallon tank truck

MAWLEY HALL

Photo : 373 Engineer General Service Regiment / National Archives

Built between 1690 and 1700, Mawley Hall followed the style of Restoration architecture and is built of brick trimmed with bath stone. This Hall, on the estate of Sir Walter Blount near Cleobury Mortimer, was occupied by units of the U.S Army from December 1943 until July 1944.

The Regimental Headquarters, Headquarters and Service Company and Motor Pool of the 1st Battalion of the 373rd Engineer General Service Regiment moved from Camp Bewdley to Mawley Hall on 10 December 1943. It was to be the Headquarters of unit's Companies engaged in the construction of the tented camps in the area. They occupied the Hall until 15 January 1944 when they were replaced by the Regimental Headquarters, Headquarters and Service Company of the 1st Battalion of the 95th Engineer General Service Regiment a coloured unit. Shortly afterwards the 95th Engineers were replaced by the Headquarters & Headquarters Detachment and Company D of the 2nd Battalion of the 1310 Engineer General Service Regiment, another coloured unit. They departed from Mawley Hall to make way for the arrival of the 221st Signal Depot Company.

The 221st Signal Depot Company departed from the New York Port of Embarkation on 31 March 1944 aboard the "Queen Elizabeth" and arrived England on 6 April 1944. The strength of the unit was 6 Officers, 2 Warrant Officers and 135 Enlisted Men.

The Bridgnorth Journal reported that a church parade at Cleobury Mortimer on Sunday, 9 July included a contingent of the U.S Army. This was probably the last public appearance of the 221st Signal Company in Cleobury as they departed from England on the 16 July for service in France.

OTHER LOCATIONS IN THE SOUTH - EAST SHROPSHIRE AREA

DHUSTONE

Clee Hill stone was widely used for road construction in U.S Army Camps, among the engineer units known to have had a small camp there was the 95th Engineer General Service Regiment.

Company A of the 1st Battalion of the 95th Engineer General Service Regiment arrived at Clee Hill during February 1944. They were quartered in pyramidal tents at Limers Lane.   Conditions there must have been unpleasant, situated over a thousand feet above sea level in winter! This was a coloured unit, and were engaged in operating the stone crusher and obtaining stone for road making at nearby camps.

Dennis Crowther, a Clee Hill resident recalls playing the harmonium at a dance at the Mission Hall, Clee Hill when 4 black soldiers entered scaring the life out of the girls present. It was probably the first time they had ever seen a black person other than in films!

CATHERTON COMMON

The 463rd AAA Automatic Weapons Battalion arrived at Crumpsbrook by motor transport from Pettypool, Cheshire on 3 May 1944.

The unit strength was 35 Officers, 3 Warrant Officers and 748 Enlisted Men, under the command of Major Robin E. Mc.Cormick.

The unit departed for Southampton, by motor transport, on 22 June 1944.

WYRE FOREST (BUTTON OAK)

The 576th Ordnance Ammunition Company were based in the Wyre Forest in the period from April to August 1944.

Ammunition was stored alongside tracks in the forest in the Button Oak area.

The duties of an Ordnance Ammunition Company were to organise and operate a Class 5 dump including the receipt, storage and the inventory of all Class 5 supplies. (ammunition, explosives and chemical agents.)

The authorised strength of the unit was 6 Officers and 180 Enlisted Men.

Sheila Lloyd was a schoolgirl during the war living at Knowles Mill on Dowles Brook. Her route to Button Oak school was along a track through the forest known as Cadbury's Lane. She remembers seeing the ammunition stored alongside this track.

Welcome Club – Bewdley

The Bewdley Welcome Club was opened on 20 February 1944 at the WVS Headquarters above the Chocolate Box in Load Street. The main function of Welcome Clubs was to bring the GIs into amicable contact with the local civilians.

The Welcome Club was a popular venue for the American troops from the Sturt Common and Kinlet Camps. The visitor's book contained names of American servicemen from 44 of the then 48 States in the U.S.A.

These entries in the Welcome Club visitor's book were probably made by men of the 95th Engineer General Service Regiment which completed construction of Kinlet Camp.

1944 photograph of the Chocolate Box, Load Street, Bewdley with the Welcome Club on the first floor.
Photo : courtesy Country Life

Town Topics by Candidus

American Army vehicles must be finding some difficulty in negotiating the roads round Bridgnorth. One went through the wall on Sunday, another had an argument with the Falcon Hotel and yet another tried conclusions with the wall by Ley's Yard.

Bridgnorth Journal,
Saturday 11 March 1944

Town Topics by Candidus

A Wolverhampton businessman coming from Bridgnorth gave an American soldier a lift. By way of being friendly he said "What do you think of Wolverhampton?"
"Waal," was the reply, "Its about half as big as Noo York General Cemetry, and twice as dead."

Bridgnorth Journal,
Saturday 27 May 1944

26 Coloured American soldiers injured

Shortly before 11p.m on Wednesday an American lorry was travelling down New Road when it failed to negotiate the bend, crashed and somersaulted into Underhill Street 30 feet below.

The lorry finished with its wheels in the air and had to be turned on its side in order that the occupants, 26 coloured soldiers, could be released.

All were injured in some degree and were taken to Bridgnorth Infirmary. There eleven received treatment, and later the whole of the party was transferred to an American military hospital in another county.

It is understood that the driver and probably two or three others received serious injuries.

At the time the lorry crashed two sisters were walking along Underhill Street in company of two American soldiers, and all four were struck by falling debris. They were removed to Bridgnorth Infirmary and the two American soldiers were later transferred to an American hospital.

Bridgnorth Journal,
Saturday 15 April 1944

APPENDIX I

Engineer General Service Regiments

Organization of 373rd Engineer General Service Regiment

The Regiment consisted of a Regimental Headquarters, a Headquarters and Service Company which supplied personnel for Regimental Headquarters, Administration Section (S-1), Engineering and Operations Section (S-3), Regimental Supply Section (S-4), and Equipment and Repair Sections. The unit carried a Medical Detachment of three doctors, two dentists and forty-four non-commissioned officers and men, a Chaplain, a Special Service Officer and an Orientation Officer, the latter carried in S-3 Section. There were two Battalions, First and Second, with their Battalion Headquarters and three line companies each:

First Battalion : Companies A, B and C
Second Battalion : Companies D, E and F.

Each Company carried a Company carried a Company Headquarters (sometimes called the Headquarters Platoon) and three line Platoons, First, Second and Third.

As an example of specialist classifications a standard line platoon carried the following :

Lieutenant. (Platoon Commander)
Staff Sergeant (Platoon Sergeant)
2 Chauffeurs
3 Sergeants (Squad Leaders)
3 Corporals (Assistant Squad Leaders)
3 Bridge Carpenters
7 General Carpenters
3 Demolition Men
3 General Electricians
3 Jack Hammer and Compressor Operators
3 General Mechanics
3 Quarry Men
3 General Riggers
1 Sheet Metal Worker or Railway Section Hand
1 Iron Worker Erector
4 Basic Privates

All these men were trained to operate as infantrymen in emergency.

Total strength on arrival at Camp Bewdley 19 November 1943 was 54 Assigned Officers and 1241 Assigned Enlisted Men.

373rd Engineer General Service Regiment
(extract from official history)

After a processing and final inspection period of two weeks, which included some amphibious training, the regiment left the United States in three trains on 31 October 1943, for Halifax, Nova Scotia, embarked immediately from trains on arrival during the night of 1 November, aboard the Cunard Liner 'Mauretania' and sailed without convoy on 2 November 1943. This liner was equipped with radar and was considered fast enough to elude enemy submarines.

The troops on board consisted of a mixture of about one half each of United States Army (Engineers, Infantry, Air Corps and Medical) and British Empire (British RAF and Navy, Canadian Air and Ground Forces, Newfoundlanders and New Zealanders). The total complement on the voyage was about 8,500 men.

The overall troop commander on ship was British Col. Lewellyn. The commander of the 373rd Engineer Regiment was troop commander of the United States forces.

Outside of some seasickness, the usual ship and boat drills, together with a most strict enforcement of blackout regulations, some anti-aircraft practice, and one temporarily unidentified passing airplane, the trip was uneventful. The liner docked at Liverpool on 9 November 1943.

That night, in the usual complete blackout maintained at that time, the regiment entrained and moved in three trains to Packington Park Camp No.5, located in the Arden Forest in North Warwickshire, on the Earl of Aylesworth's estate, arriving there before daylight on 10 November. Thanks to the excellent work done by the advance detachment under Captains James W.Elmore, CE and William Ernsting, Jr.,CE, the kind assistance of British Army forces stationed adjoining, and help loaned by the 347th Engineer G.S Regiment, commanded by Col. Harry Hulen,CE, barracks built by British carpenters were ready and battalion messes started.

The regiment, having been allocated to Western Base Section, SOS, USA,through Col. C.H.Chorpening, CE, at that time Base Section Engineer, received orders to construct certain camps for concentration of invasion forces. As soon as equipment was received it was decided to move to a location nearer the center of work. On 19 November, all troops (less Second Platoon of Company F, 2nd Lt. Lawrence M.Downes, CE, commanding, which departed for Camp Crookston, Scotland, on a construction mission) were moved under their own organic transportation by shuttle system to a recently completed camp, Bewdley No.2, near Kidderminster, Worcestershire. After setting up Headquarters here it was found necessary, after reconnaissance, to fan out the line companies to their various sites of work, there to set up their bivouac tented construction camps adjoining their projects. This was accomplished immediately and Regimental Headquarters, Headquarters and Service Company and Motor Pool were moved to Mawley Hall on the estate of Sir Walter Blount, near Cleobury Mortimer, Shropshire.

Camp construction on beautiful manorial estates was started and continued until the latter part of January 1944, at which time work of a higher priority and demanding an organization of heavy construction background, namely the extension of the storage yards and depot, near Barry, necessitated moving the Second Battalion to that site. Their camp work was taken over by the 95th Engineer G.S Regiment (coloured). The First Battalion was also moved to start and organize new projects further north; and likewise, when this battalion was ordered into final training for the invasion, their unfinished work was assumed by the 95th and 1310th Engineer Regiments.

373rd Engineer General Service Regiment

Commendations

OFFICE OF BASE SECTION ENGINEER
WESTERN BASE SECTION
SOS U.S. ARMY
A.P.O.515

12 Dec 1943

Dear Colonel Bell,

*** Extract ***

While I regretted the fact that it was not possible for me to spend more time with you and your units, during my recent visit, I saw enough to convince me that your regiment is tackling its construction tasks in a businesslike and proper manner. I was impressed with the evidences everywhere of aggressive, positive and efficient action.

It is my confident expectation that the 373rd Engineers will attain a record of performance that will make it outstanding in this Base Section and in the theater.

Sincerely yours,

/s/ C.H.CHORPENING
Colonel, Corps of Engineers,
Base Section Engineer

Draft below prepared by Troops Division, OCE ETOUSA, based on a report of Camouflage Officer, OCE, dated 17 January 1944, concerning his inspection of 12 January 1944. Quotations refer to Coton, Gatacre and Chyknell Camps respectively.

Training Memorandum.   HVC/jk
SUBJECT: Camouflage and Construction.   ETOUSA 1404

1. (a) Recently construction work in one Base Section was inspected by the Camouflage Officer, from the Office of the Chief Engineer. *The work being done by one unit was so outstanding, both from the construction viewpoint as well as the camouflage viewpoint* that quotations from the report of the Camouflage Officer are given below:

*** extract ***

2. The construction procedure in the regiment was excellent, both for Engineering efficiency and for speed. The finishing of each portion of the work, the good housekeeping and orderly layout and procedure were found to aid construction efficiency as well as to aid in camouflage.

3. The procedure of this unit indicated that speed of construction was not necessarily obtained by promiscuous cutting and scarring of the ground, leaving piles of debris, and thoughtless disregard to more common orderly military precautions.

4. Recent constructions regarding camouflage, if followed with intelligence, should aid in construction and in military efficiency.

373rd Engineer General Service Regiment

"Phoenix" Project

While processed and waiting to proceed to the marshalling area for embarkation, telegraphic orders were received by the Regimental Commander ordering him to report to the Office of the Chief Engineer in London.

It developed that the temporary breakwater protection for landing and docking at 'Omaha' and 'Utah' beaches had become acute due to storms breaking up the artificial harbours constructed with 'Phoenixes' sometimes called 'Mulberries'. Immediate replacements were given the highest priority by Supreme Headquarters Allied Expeditionary Force (SHAEF).

The British Ministry of War requested aid from the U.S Corps of Engineers. The work was carried on under the Office of the U.S Chief of Engineers, Major C.R Moore, for the British Ministry of Supply. The Commanding Officer of the 373rd Engineers, who was made Project Engineer and Group Commander, was directly responsible for the construction to the Chief of Engineers, ETO.

A 'Phoenix' consisted of a reinforced concrete box, sectioned internally (cellular) for strength, approximately 204 feet long by 62 feet wide by 60 feet high, with a 6 foot offset gangway around the perimeter at the 28 foot elevation, the unit being equipped with a system of valves for flooding and sinking. The bottoms were 15 inches thick, the sides 12 inches thick up to the 28 foot level and from there 9 inches. Each unit contained approximately 4,000 cubic yards of concrete and 700 tons of reinforcing steel.

Three units were constructed by the 373rd Engineers.

Unit 190 at Tilbury Docks by Companies D and E.
Unit 191 at Globe Wharf by Companies A and B.
Unit 192 at Globe Wharf by Companies C and F.

Imperial War Museum H40320
A Phoenix breakwater under construction at Tilbury Docks, 1944

95th Engineer General Service Regiment

This coloured unit arrived mid January 1944 to continue with the construction of the summer tented camps due to the departure of the 373rd General Service Regiment for higher priority tasks.

They were quartered as follows:

Headquarters ………………………….... Mawley Hall
Headquarters Service Company ……... . Mawley Hall
1st Battalion HQ & HQ Detachment …. Mawley Hall
1st Battalion, Company A ……………. Dhustone
1st Battalion, Company B ……….…… Sturt Common
1st Battalion, Company C …………….. Kinlet
2nd Battalion HQ & HQ Detachment … Stanley Hall
2nd Battalion, Company D …………..... Kinlet
2nd Battalion, Company E …………..... Davenport House
2nd Battalion, Company F ……………. Gatacre Hall

The unit was assisted by the 413rd Dumper Truck Company, a coloured unit, based at Gatacre Hall.

In addition to completing the construction of the tented camps the 95th Engineer General Service Regiment also widened and straightened narrow lanes in the area and strengthened bridges to allow the passage of U.S Army vehicles.

1310th Engineer General Service Regiment

Company D of the 2nd Battalion of the 1310th Engineer Regiment arrived at Mawley Hall towards the end of March 1944 to construct a tented camp in the grounds of the house. Again this was a coloured unit.

APPENDIX II
90th Infantry Division

Commanding Officer : Brigadier General Jay W. McKelvie

The T-O on the division's insignia stood for Texas and Oklahoma, for originally those were the states the men were drawn from. Later, however, the division drew its men from every state in the U.S.A, and the T-O came to represent "Tough 'Ombres."

In March 1944, the unit moved to its staging area at Camp Kilmer, New Jersey. On 22 March the troops entrained for New York City. There they boarded ships and the following day sailed out of New York Harbor bound for England.

On 8 April , Easter Sunday, they arrived at Liverpool. After debarking the troops loaded immediately on trains and moved to the Midlands of England.

The Division Headquarters was set up at King Edwards School in Birmingham. The Division's Infantry Regiments, with the exception of the 359th, were quartered in tented camps in South East Shropshire at Sturt Common, Kinlet Hall, Coton Hall and Gatacre Hall. The Division's Special Troops were also at Sturt Common. The Field Artillery Battalions attached to the 90th Infantry Division were based at Davenport House, near Bridgnorth. The 359th Infantry Regiment were quartered outside Shropshire (at Leominster and Stanage Park (Willey Moor) near Knighton.)

Intensive training was begun immediately with stress being placed on speed marches and on forced marches with heavy loads of weapons and ammunition. They also practised infantry action including village fighting, obstacle courses and extended drill designed to move squads, platoons and companies about with the men spread out as if they were under artillery and small arms fire.

During their stay, the men were granted short passes to nearby towns. For two months, trucks drove soldiers every evening and Sundays to Kidderminster and to the City of   Birmingham. Others went to the nearby town of Bewdley where the local atmosphere as well as ale was absorbed.

Towards the end of May the 90th Infantry Division moved to embarkation camps in South Wales near to the ports of Newport and Cardiff. Loading into military transport ships commenced on 2 June and the division set sail on 4 June. On 5 June the ships dropped anchor in the Bristol Channel near Swansea where the rest of the convoy assembled. By 2.00 a.m on 6 June, D-Day the convoy was under way towards France, following a route close to the coast of England, arriving off Utah Beach mid morning of 8 June.

During its fight for the liberation of Europe the 90th Infantry Division suffered heavy casualties. Nearly 4,000 were killed in action or died of wounds and over 14,000 wounded in action.

ORGANIZATION CHART

90th INFANTRY DIVISION

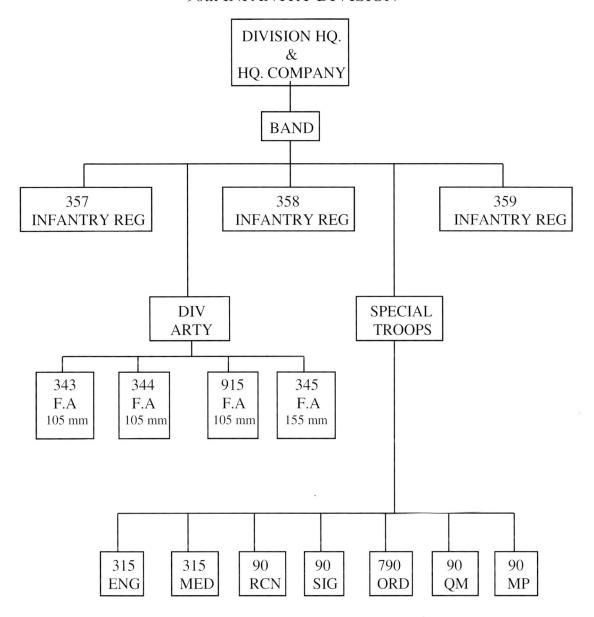

Strength of Infantry Regiment ….. 3,118 men
Strength of Medium Field Artillery Battalion (155 mm howitzer) … 527 men
Strength of Light Field Artillery Battalion (105 mm howitzer) …….. 509 men
Total authorized strength of division, including special troops …. 14,000 men

APPENDIX III

Since the publication of " The U.S Army at Camp Bewdley and locations in the Wyre Forest" was published additional information has come to hand and is included in this section.

48th Field Hospital

Commanding Officer : Lt. Col. Robert R. Hoagland

Strength of unit : 22 Officers, 18 Nurses and 190 Enlisted Men.

The following is an extract from the unit's official history :

We boarded "HMS Arundel Castle" in New York Port and sailed at 2 bells –0900– 7 April 1944. "The lady with the torch" slipped by quickly and we were out of the harbor.

Ships had been leaving the harbor all morning, and in no time at all we seemed to be part of a large assemblage of boats to port and starboard and stretching out for many miles.

Eating was something everybody had trouble with. Some just weren't hungry, and for those who had an appetite there were only two meals a day being prepared. The crowded conditions of the ship made it impossible to serve more, and as it was, the chow lines for the second meal began forming soon after the first meal was finished.

"Abandon ship" drills were held every day. The captain spoke every morning over the public address system, and offered a prayer for a safe voyage. Good Friday and Easter Sunday services were celebrated on board ship.

We had been assigned to our unit a number of small rooms on "A" and "B" decks for the nurses and officers and a large newly equipped compartment below "D" deck and as far "aft" as you can get in a ship, for the enlisted men. These quarters were better than were available to some of the troops on the ship. The compartment had been converted from the ship's refrigerator, therefore, we had rather frigid ventilation. It was quite useful, however, for the quarters were overcrowded and, without good ventilation, would have been unbearable.

Time hung heavy on everyone's hands with cards and dice being the prevalent dispersers of gloom.

The first land to be sighted after leaving the States, was the northern tip of Ireland. This was on 15 April. Later on the same day we sighted the western banks of Scotland, and early in the morning of 16 April we steamed into the anchorage at the mouth of the Firth of Clyde. Late that afternoon we sailed up the Firth and that night, near midnight, we debarked at Glasgow, Scotland. We went immediately to a London, Midland and Scottish train. On 17 April, at 1345, we arrived in Kidderminster, Worcestershire, England. From the train we went directly to our area.

There was only one building in the area, a newly constructed mess hall. The entire unit was given billets in private homes nearby.

There were no attempts to follow any prescribed schedule at any time during April. Our voyage in the early part of the month made this unnecessary and the remainder of the month we spent becoming adjusted to our new surroundings.

England is a beautiful country, all will agree to that. The men were not closely restricted as far as travelling was concerned, and those who took advantage of it can appreciate the beauty of the English countryside in the spring.

Being quartered in the homes of Englishmen gave us the opportunity of English home life, although it couldn't be declared normal under war restrictions. They were, however, hospitable and well mannered hosts.

The immortalized English pub had all the flavor and atmosphere given to it in poems, pictures and stories. Without any doubt, it became the most popular pastime of a majority of the Americans.

....

The 48th Field Hospital mess hall. To the English it was "The American Canteen."

The 48th Field Hospital were billeted in houses similar to those in the photograph, in Birchfield Road and Greatfield Road.

A favourite pub visited by the men of the 48th was the "Castle" in Park Lane. Another recreational pursuit was visits to the Public Baths in Castle Road, Kidderminster.

Training sessions were held in Habberley Valley, each platoon separately spent at least 5 days setting up the hospital in darkness and inclement weather.

On 17 June, 12 Officers, 14 Nurses and 22 Enlisted men from the 4th Auxillary Group were attached to the unit.

During July 1944 a Garden Party was held at 'Oakfield', on Bewdley Hill, organised by the British Legion (Women's Section). Lt. Winifred Johnson, a 48th Field Hospital Nurse, distributed the prizes.

All the personnel departed from Kidderminster on 10 July 1944.

Photo : John Frampton

A children's party being held at the former mess halls of the 48th Field Hospital in Birchfield Road.
Photograph taken after the departure of the U.S troops.